Sean Connolly

W
FRANKLIN WATTS
LONDON • SYDNEY

 An Appleseed Editions book

First published in 2005 by Franklin Watts

Paperback edition 2007

Franklin Watts
338 Euston Road, London NW1 3BH

Franklin Watts Australia
Level 17/207 Kent Street, Sydney, NSW 2000

© 2005 Appleseed Editions

Appleseed Editions Ltd
Well House, Friars Hill, Guestling, East Sussex TN35 4ET

Designed by Helen James

ISBN 978 0 7496 7648 3

Dewey Classification: 331.01' 1

A CIP catalogue for this book is available from the British Library

Photographs by Corbis (Archivo Iconografico, S.A., Bettmann, Michael Freeman, Hulton–Deutsch Collection, Michael S. Lewis, Reuters, Schenectady Museum; Hall of Electrical History Foundation, Flip Schulke, Paul A. Souders, Selwyn Tait/CORBIS SYGMA, Peter Turnley, Patrick Ward), Getty Images (AFP, MPI, STR/AFP)

Printed in China

Franklin Watts is a division of Hachette Children's Books

Contents

Wrongs and Rights

People often talk about the stress of their jobs. They refer to all kinds of problems they face at work – meeting performance targets, getting projects done before a tight deadline, keeping track of money and expensive equipment or even getting on with colleagues. These pressures are common, and some are unavoidable.

But most of them pale in comparison with the stress and real danger faced by workers in the past. Workers once had to worry about being fired if they were injured on the job. They sometimes lost up to half of their weekly pay for going to the toilet without permission. And children were forced to work up to 14 hours a day for little or no pay. For most, the only alternative to working in such conditions was begging or living in a **workhouse**.

Hard-won Victories

Over the past two centuries, many people have bravely fought to remove these terrible obstacles to earning a living safely. They have met opposition not only from employers, but also from governments that have passed and enforced laws to strengthen employers' positions. One by one, though, victories have been achieved, providing today's workers with rights such as sick pay, paid holidays, **pensions** and the opportunity to find work regardless of race, religion or gender.

New Challenges

The world that created the rights that so many workers now enjoy is changing quickly. Experts search for the right term to describe the working world today – 'the new economy', 'the information age', 'the communications revolution'. They find the working world difficult to define because so many of the things that were taken for granted as recently as three decades ago have changed dramatically.

Where workers once fell into two main categories – farming and industrial – now there are new categories developing all the time. Who, even in the 1980s, had heard of web site design, working in **call centres**, or **telecommuting**? Yet that is what millions of people now do for a living. They are unlikely to lose a thumb on a rotating saw, develop lung disease from coal dust or go blind from close needlework – 'traditional' risks covered by today's range of labour laws. They may, however, face new risks that endanger their mental health, earning power or **job security**. It will be the task of reformers in the 21st century to identify these new risks and to make sure that today's rights at work keep pace with the changing workplace.

Children as young as four years old were put to work scooping oysters from their shells at this Louisiana shellfish company in the early 1900s.

Examples from History

Archaeologists believe that the earliest human beings fended for themselves, looking for their own food and shelter and protecting their families. Later, these early humans formed small communities in which people worked as teams to find food, share shelter and protect one another. The term 'rights at work' had no real meaning in primitive societies, because everyone worked for the community as a whole, whether as a hunter, planter or caregiver.

The next big step forwards was the creation of permanent settlements, in which people grew crops and built real homes in place of temporary shelters. Tools, remains of slaughtered animals and cave paintings all suggest that the roots of our modern villages, towns and cities developed in these early times.

The Price of Civilization

Although it might seem that the concept of rights at work is a modern idea, the history of the struggles of workers actually goes back thousands of years to the time when primitive communities began to give way to civilized societies. With the rise of civilizations, rights at work began to take on some significance.

Late 12th-century sculptures at Angkor Thom, Cambodia, show how slaves were tied together and put to work in the imperial city.

Egyptian Strike

The first recorded strike took place in ancient Egypt in about 1150 BC. Egyptian labourers of that time received part of their pay in the form of grain. A food shortage meant that workers were forced to go without pay (or food). During one such shortage, construction workers at the temples of Deir el-Medina, a settlement in central Egypt, stopped working in protest. They occupied the vaults where they had been working until the vizier – the highest government official – promised to make up for the shortage. But when the grain did not arrive, the workers resumed their strike. Finally, the governor arrived with grain and copper to pay the workers. They went back to work without suffering any punishment, even though Egyptian law forbade such strikes.

One mark of the development of a civilized society was its ability to produce more than enough food, leaving some 'spare' workers (who had originally been food-gatherers). These workers were then free to build and decorate houses and temples, work on paintings and sculptures and record the comings and goings of society. As societies became civilized, people began to work for others – whether rulers, priests or simply other inhabitants – for the first time. They used the money they earned in this way to provide for their basic needs, including food, land and housing, rather than producing these items on their own.

A wall painting from around 1300 BC shows Egyptian slaves working in fields during the annual grain harvest.

At the bottom of the social ladder in these early civilizations were slaves, who were considered the property of their owners. They had no choice about the work they did or where they lived – in short, they had no control over their own lives. European societies in the **Middle Ages** generally had abandoned slavery, but the **feudal system** limited the freedom of most labourers, who had to work for the local nobleman. Most of these labourers worked on farms, but new groups of workers, known as guilds, developed in towns and cities. These groups were formed mainly as a way of teaching young people certain jobs such as carpentry or building, but they also encouraged workers in these trades to

A young man learns the art of alchemy (an early form of chemistry aimed at changing common stone into gold or silver) while his master reads out a recipe.

reach agreements. Members of a guild would often elect leaders who would persuade feudal rulers to exclude non-members from important business activities, such as selling goods for profit, thereby strengthening the guild's control over its trade. The formation of guilds eventually led workers to realize that there was strength in numbers and that together they could achieve far more than they could on their own.

By the late Middle Ages, other professional groups began to develop as a way of pushing for improved working conditions and pay. The first of these was formed by midwives (people who deliver babies) in Regensburg, Germany, in 1452. Over the next few centuries, other groups would explore the 'tools' that workers' groups could use to achieve their goals. The most basic of these was the strike, in which workers refused to work, leading to a loss of income for their employers.

Early American Strikes

Workers in Colonial America saw the benefits of uniting from the earliest times. Unlike workers in Europe, they had fewer longstanding ties with their villages or local employers. In 1636, just 16 years after the Pilgrims landed in Massachusetts, fishermen in Maine **mutinied** over poor working conditions. **Indentured servants** used the strike weapon in several southern colonies in the mid-17th century, while New York City later saw a number of disruptive strikes – including the **carters'** strikes of 1677 and 1684, as well as a bakers' strike in 1741. In 1792, Philadelphia shoemakers formed the first local **union** organized for **collective bargaining**, which formed the foundation of labour rights goals for the next two centuries.

8

Worker Unity

An English rebellion in 1381 gave the world an idea of how powerful workers could be if they united. **Peasants** resented a new tax imposed by the king to pay for a war with France. In previous centuries, they would have grudgingly agreed to pay the tax, knowing that they could lose their livelihood if they displeased the king or powerful landowners. But only three decades earlier, the Black Death, a deadly disease, had swept through Europe. About a third of England's population had died during that outbreak. Those peasants who had survived were now in a surprisingly strong position. With far fewer workers to replace them, the peasants could afford to protest. Led by an ex-soldier named Wat Tyler, they rampaged across southeast England and marched on London. There they were strong enough to force King Richard II to abandon the tax. Although Tyler was eventually killed – and many of the rebels executed – the king chose not to reimpose the tax because he was afraid of provoking another threat to his power. The Peasants' Revolt, as it became known, remained a powerful memory in English minds. Labour leaders in later centuries would cite it as proof that workers could band together to achieve a shared goal.

Wat Tyler was killed by William Walworth, mayor of London, on June 15, 1381, while he tried to bargain for improved working conditions.

A New Dimension

The struggle for rights at work really became organized and recognized in the 19th century. Although there had been scattered moves to organize workers in specific trades or localities before that time, these efforts – and the benefits they brought – were isolated. The wide-scale development of industry across western Europe and North America changed all that.

The **Industrial Revolution**, which had begun in the 1700s in Great Britain and then spread to other countries, transformed the way in which goods were produced. Large factories could manufacture goods by the hundreds or thousands, when only a few decades before, individual workers had produced the same goods one by one. Factories needed many workers to keep the machines in constant operation. Many people left rural areas – where new farming machinery had eliminated many traditional jobs – and moved to cities and towns in search of work.

Workers at this manufacturing shop in Lynn, Massachusetts, operated machines driven by long belts suspended from the ceiling.

Results of a Revolution

The Industrial Revolution began in Britain, where many decades of peace had left the people with money to buy manufactured goods. With the rising population using up most of Britain's charcoal, manufacturers turned to coal to power their factories. Coal, in turn, allowed manufacturers to develop steam-powered machines. These machines were put to use initially in the **textile** industry, but factory owners soon saw that other products, such as tools, cutlery, railway tracks and even household decorations, could be made in large quantities at a relatively low cost. The new factories created to produce these products – in Britain and in other countries with developing industries – drew many people from rural villages to the towns and cities where the factories were located. In 1800, for example, only three per cent of the world's population lived in towns or cities. That figure had more than doubled by 1850 and more than doubled again by the beginning of the 20th century.

Difficult Conditions

Although the raw materials that the factories needed – coal, steam and running water – were inexpensive, this didn't mean that workers were paid well. Most workers in factories, mines and textile mills worked long hours in extremely dangerous conditions for less than a pound a week. Many died in industrial accidents caused by poor safety precautions and the fatigue of working such long hours. Exhausted workers lost fingers and hands in the spinning machinery. Miners and many factory workers contracted silicosis, a lung disease. People manufacturing matches often developed bone diseases because of their constant contact with the chemical phosphorus. Prolonged exposure to soot increased the risk of skin cancer among chimney sweeps. Those who were injured and unable to continue working received no disability payments.

To make matters worse, the poorest workers in most societies had no real voice in government because only the wealthiest men had the right to vote. Workers could not bring their grievances and concerns to the wider public in order to push through new laws ensuring safe working conditions. The answer lay in renewing a tradition that had its roots in the Middle Ages and even earlier – grouping together to form powerful organizations devoted to improving working conditions. It was against this background that the first modern trade unions were born.

William Cuffay

British workers' rights activist William Cuffay (1788–1870) was the son of a naval cook and former slave. As a child, Cuffay became an apprentice tailor. At first, he held conservative views and opposed the formation of trade unions. Reluctantly, he eventually joined the local branch of the tailors' union just before it went on strike in 1834. Angered after losing his job in this dispute, Cuffay was won over to the cause of unions and workers' rights. He believed that workers – who at that time could not vote in Britain – needed to be represented in Parliament.

In the early 1840s, Cuffay became an important spokesman for the **Chartists**. At the famous Kennington Common meeting in the spring of 1848, some Chartists urged him to lead an armed uprising in London. Cuffay refused, but a police informer named Powell – who had infiltrated the Chartist movement – provided evidence against Cuffay and other leading Chartists. Cuffay protested his innocence and accused Powell of lying throughout a long trial. He also questioned the legality of the trial itself, since he did not believe that he was being tried 'by his equals' – the jury members were all property owners who were likely to be against the Chartist movement. In the end, Cuffay was sentenced to prison in Tasmania, Australia, for 21 years. Although all political prisoners in Tasmania were pardoned in 1856, Cuffay remained there and continued his campaign in Australia. He died there in poverty in 1870.

'I say you have no right to sentence me. Although the trial has lasted a long time, it has not been a fair trial, and my request to have a fair trial – to be tried by my equals – has not been complied with. I am not anxious for martyrdom, but after what I have endured this week, I feel that I could bear any punishment proudly, even to the **scaffold**.'

William Cuffay, after his trial in 1848.

The Tolpuddle Martyrs

The tiny village of Tolpuddle in southwest England was the site of a memorable event in the history of workers' rights. In 1833, a group of workers formed a lodge of the Friendly Society of Agricultural Labourers in Tolpuddle. They planned to work together to increase their low wages. As part of their initiation, they had to swear before a picture of a skeleton that they would never disclose the union's secrets.

British Prime Minister Lord Melbourne and his government opposed trade unions. They supported the arrest and trial of six of the Tolpuddle union members. The men were charged with administering unlawful oaths – a reference to the skeleton initiation – but the unofficial charge was trying to organize farm labourers in a trade union. The six men were convicted, and in March 1834, they were sentenced to seven years in a penal colony in Australia.

The trial was widely reported in British newspapers, and many people were outraged at the conviction and sentence of the men, who became known as the 'Tolpuddle Martyrs'. More than 250,000 people signed a petition supporting the martyrs and 30,000 people marched to Whitehall – the heart of British government in London – to add their support. Sensing real unrest and fearing violence, the government backed down and agreed to send the men home from Australia. Tolpuddle became a place of pilgrimage for trade unionists, and the tree under which the martyrs met – now only a stump – is one of the most famous landmarks in British trade union history.

Trade unionists acknowledge their debt to the Tolpuddle Martyrs in a march through the English village of Tolpuddle in 2002.

Focus on Children

The birth of trade unions gave workers their first real chance to improve working conditions. The strike was a powerful weapon in pushing forward their demands, even if factory owners often called on police forces to disrupt demonstrators. But many of the factories that developed during the Industrial Revolution relied on an even cheaper source of labour – children – to make a profit.

As with so many areas of industrial development, Great Britain was at the forefront of using children in industry. Poverty drove many British families to send their children to work. Even the income from both parents was not enough to support large families, which often had six or more children. Factory owners often rounded up orphans and children from poor families to work in mills and other manufacturing centres. In return, they paid for the children's food and lodging. These children – some as young as five or six – often worked up to 16 hours a day, with no one to look after their health or well-being. But no matter how bad their working conditions were, they knew that the alternatives – begging on the streets or going into a workhouse – were no better.

Figures that Speak for Themselves

In 1833, there were about 6,900 people employed in the busy cotton mills of Lancashire, England, with the oldest aged 61. But the single largest group – making up 2,291 of the workers – were boys and girls between the ages of 11 and 16. The plight of these and other young workers prompted calls for changes in child labour laws in Britain and around the world.

Other countries followed Britain's lead. During the first half of the 19th century, for example, children between the ages of seven and twelve made up a third of the overall workforce in United States factories. Similar conditions were common in Canada, continental Europe and Australia.

Causes for Concern

Unlike adult workers, children had little or no chance to organize themselves in groups such as unions. It took the perseverance and compassion of a number of adult reformers to publicize and improve children's working conditions.

In order to bring about changes, many reformers in the United States focused on education. They warned that children who worked full-time received little or no education and would grow up to be **illiterate**. To prevent this, reformers called for education laws. Massachusetts lawmakers took the first step in 1836 when they passed a law barring employers from hiring any child under the age of 15 who had completed less than three months of education in the previous year. Other states adopted similar provisions.

Nearly all American child labour laws were the responsibility of the individual states. Some states insisted that no one under the age of 12 could work in factories. Others set a one-hour limit to children's working days. But as American industry boomed in the late 19th century, it became more difficult to enforce child labour laws.

Boys at work in a Georgia cotton mill, in America around 1910. The work of photographers like Lewis Wickes Hine drew public attention to the dangers of child labour.

'The parents rouse them in the morning and receive them tired and exhausted after the day has closed; they see them droop and sicken and, in many cases, become cripples and die before they reach their prime; and they do all this because they must otherwise starve. It is a mockery to contend that these parents have a choice. They choose the lesser evil and reluctantly resign their offspring to the captivity and pollution of the mill.'

British reformer Michael Sadler, describing child labour conditions to the House of Commons, March 16, 1832.

Getting the Message Across

Working people – and especially working children – had little opportunity to publicize their demands for better conditions in the 19th century. Instead, they had to rely on the tireless work of social reformers. Henry Hetherington (1792–1849), the son of a London tailor, was a shining example. Hetherington trained as a printer and, by his early 20s, had started his own printing and publishing company. He began publishing **radical** newspapers that called for improved educational and working conditions for children. One of these papers, *The Poor Man's Guardian,* was selling 22,000 copies a week in the early 1830s.

Hetherington's efforts often landed him in trouble with the law, which acted against anti-government publications. He faced frequent fines, spent two short periods in prison, and even had his printing presses seized and destroyed in 1835. Despite these obstacles, he continued to champion the causes of child labour reform and improved working conditions. He helped publicize the Chartist message of employment reform and was a vocal critic of the government until his death. Two thousand people attended his funeral in 1849.

British opinion about child labour was also beginning to change, thanks to newspaper accounts of working conditions and investigations led by Parliament. Reformers such as Michael Sadler and Henry Hetherington had championed the cause of child labour reforms since the early 1830s. Their efforts bore fruit decades later with new laws controlling conditions for working children. An 1868 law set the minimum age for employees at ten. Children between the ages of ten and 14 could work only on alternate days and no more than a half-day on Saturday. Like the United States, Britain concentrated on education as a way of helping children escape from the trap of working in factories. The Education Act of 1870 established state-funded primary schools for all British children for the first time.

A British poster from the early 1900s helps draw attention to the dangerous conditions faced by child workers.

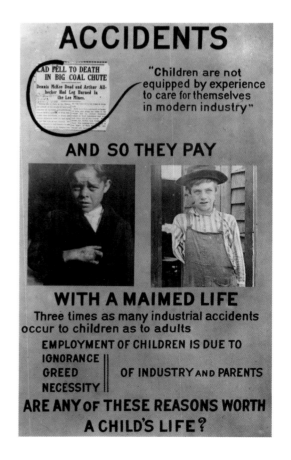

16

Mother Jones

One of the most tireless campaigners for working rights was Mary Harris, known as 'Mother Jones'. She overcame personal tragedy – losing her husband and four small children to a yellow fever epidemic when she was 37 years old – to become one of America's leading voices on trade unions and rights at work. She was an active public figure for nearly six decades after that, adding her voice to campaigns even when she was in her 90s.

Mother Jones took a special interest in working children. She believed that child labour was cruel and wrong but that, as long as it existed, children should be protected and given the chance to be educated properly. In one of her most famous protests, she led a large group of children from striking families in Pennsylvania to the home of President Theodore Roosevelt at Oyster Bay, New York. In a letter to the president, she wrote: 'I have espoused the cause of the labouring class in general and of suffering children in particular. The children [must be] freed from the workshops and sent to school.'

'Hear the wail of the children, who never have a chance to go to school but work 10 to 11 hours a day in the textile mills.'

Mary Harris ('Mother Jones'), during a march of mill children, July 28, 1903.

Eleven-year-old Nanni Coleson earned three dollars a week sewing stockings in this North Carolina factory in 1914.

Women's Struggles

The movement for improved workers' rights was dominated by men at its beginning. In the 18th and early 19th centuries, women had few rights in any country, even though many of them worked. In Britain, for example, even the wealthiest women were considered to be virtually the property of their husbands. Poorer women, working in mills or as seamstresses, could hardly expect equality with men. Other countries with British influence, such as Australia and Canada, based their laws on the British system, so women were also considered to be almost owned by their husbands. It wasn't surprising that working conditions for women in these countries were harsh and unregulated.

Conditions for women in the United States were not any better. As American industry developed in the 19th century, women, like children, were seen as an inexpensive alternative to adult male employees.

Women working in this Spanish cotton mill in the early 1900s put in long hours in noisy, dangerous conditions.

And, like children, women had fewer opportunities to join together to improve their position in the workplace. To make matters worse, many women working in northern American factories were immigrants from central and eastern Europe who had little command of the English language; in the South, many factory spaces were filled by ex-slaves. Conditions were hardly ideal for organizing a movement to champion the rights of women workers.

Conditions for seamstresses in this New York dress factory had improved by about 1890: they could sit while they operated sewing machines.

The British Position

British women lagged behind men in organizing for better rights at work. Women were banned from becoming members of many British craft unions, which acted on behalf of workers in most manufacturing jobs. Even by 1914, more than 90 per cent of British women workers were not part of a trade union. Those who were union members were linked mainly with the textile industry, and the rest were scattered among teaching, clerical and shop workers' unions.

Rather than looking to men – and the wider trade union movement – for assistance, women workers found more success with **philanthropic** women who were prepared to support their cause. Groups such as the Women's Protective and **Provident** League (later the Women's Trade Union League), founded in 1874, helped raise support and generate publicity for women's rights at work.

The Match Girls' Strike

One of the most influential events in British employment history was the Match Girls' Strike of 1888. The strike strengthened women's involvement in the wider union movement, and it publicized some of the terrible conditions that working women faced in Great Britain. It began when Annie Besant, a leading social reformer, learned of the harsh conditions endured by employees at the Bryant & May match factory in London. She interviewed Bryant & May employees and learned that they worked 14-hour days and were fined up to a day's pay for small offences such as talking or going to the toilet without permission.

On June 23, 1888, Besant wrote an article in her newspaper, *The Link*, entitled 'White Slavery in London'. In it, she publicized the dangerous working conditions and harsh penalties faced by the 'match girls'. Bryant & May responded by forcing workers to sign a statement saying that they were satisfied with their working conditions. Some of those who refused to sign were fired, prompting all 1,400 Bryant & May workers to go on on strike.

The Match Girls' Strike divided British opinion. Some leading figures, including Catherine Booth of the Salvation Army and playwright George Bernard Shaw, added their voices to Besant's in support of the strike. Besant called for a **boycott** of Bryant & May products. Other voices, including the influential *Times* newspaper, blamed rabble-rousers for stirring up trouble.

The factory workers formed a union, and Besant became its leader. After three weeks of pressure – and lost profits – the company backed down. It agreed to re-employ those workers who had been fired, and it abandoned its harsh system of fines. The match girls returned to work in triumph. Following the success of the match girls, other groups of workers – male and female alike – decided to form unions to push for better working conditions.

Annie Besant, whose reporting triggered the Match Girls' Strike of 1888.

Progress and Barriers

Despite the obstacles facing them, American women managed to begin organizing themselves just as men were doing. One of the first trade unions for women, the United Tailoresses of New York, was founded in 1825. It showed that women were capable of uniting to push for better conditions, and it became an example for other working women in America and the world at large.

Nevertheless, women continued to lag behind men in most areas of workers' rights, largely because they could not influence lawmaking by voting. Conditions improved in the early 20th century, when women in most countries gained that right. But even today, the struggle for women's equality in the workplace is far from over. Women in most countries continue to earn less than men who do the same job. Part of the problem lies in people's attitudes. Many men – and some women – believe that 'a woman's place is in the home' rather than in the workplace. They vote for politicians who share these views, slowing the pace of progress for women who work, or who would like to do so.

Members of the America's National Women's Trade Union League meet at their second convention, held in Chicago in 1909.

21

Working Together

Unlike some causes, the campaign for rights at work has had no single leader or earth-changing event to give it momentum. Instead, it has been a broad-based movement in which people have looked to successes in other types of work or in other places as examples of how to conduct their own campaigns.

The United Automobile Workers became one of America's most powerful unions following successful strikes in the mid-1930s.

Upton Sinclair's tireless campaigning led to improved working conditions and pure food laws in the US.

Many of the rights that today's workers take for granted – the eight-hour day, paid holidays, safe working conditions – came about because of the tireless efforts of activists who struggled to establish them during the 19th century. Their successes inspired other working people, and they also inspired journalists, writers and other public figures to push even harder for rights at work. It was a time of big business – and big profits – but it was also a period when working people realized that they could achieve clear-cut goals if they united and persevered. Match girls in London, textile workers in Britain and America and even cowboys in Texas knew that their individual struggles could eventually benefit others.

Hardie and the Labour Party

The British general election of 1892 saw the victory of James Keir Hardie, an independent labour candidate representing a poor industrial district of London. Hardie was a committed trade unionist who believed that the many different labour groups in Britain should join together as one political force. He shocked many members of Parliament – who traditionally wore top hats and long black coats – by entering Parliament wearing a cloth cap and tweed suit. Hardie's willingness to oppose tradition eventually bore fruit when, in 1900, Britain's trade unions voted to form a political party. The result was the Labour Party, which was officially established in 1906.

As a child Hardie worked 12 hour days in coal mines. He pressed for labour reforms once he entered Parliament.

The stakes were very high during this period of economic growth. Just as workers had begun to organize themselves widely in trade unions and other labour organizations, businesses were also banding together – especially in the United States.

Beginning in the 1880s, some US company owners persuaded shareholders (members of the public who own a part, or share, of a company) to allow a group of people called 'trustees' to act on their behalf. These trustees eventually had control over a number of companies that had previously competed with each other. Now, they behaved like one very large company, which could dictate the way an entire industry could operate without competition. These large companies could decide on who supplied goods for an industry, how much the public would pay for the finished product and what sort of rights workers within the industry should have. Luckily for workers, this new style of business was very unpopular with the public. A series of 'anti-trust laws' – many still in effect – worked against these 'trusts', but workers realized the need to organize themselves across entire industries to protect their rights.

The Cowboy Strike

Most people associate strikes with factories or mines, but an event in 1883 showed how widespread the campaign for workers' rights had become. That year, the cowboys of west Texas went on strike. They were unhappy with the working arrangements set in place by some of the ranch owners. Many of the owners were from the East and saw ranching as simply a business – and a way to make money. They stopped many practices that previously had been common, such as allowing cowboys to graze their own cattle on the ranches. In March 1883, about 325 cowboys went on strike against five of these ranches. The dispute gained national publicity but, over the course of nearly three months, the striking cowboys were ground down. Owners refused to concede any of the major issues, but they offered a small pay increase. Many cowboys, worried about money, decided to return to work. While the strike failed to achieve its main goals, it showed that workers in any type of employment could strike to achieve or maintain their rights.

African-American and foreign-born farm workers press for unity at a 1936 labour meeting in New Jersey.

The Shorter Workday

Throughout much of the 19th century, labourers in many types of work were required to spend up to 14 hours a day at their jobs. Pressure for an eight-hour workday began among Australian workers in 1856. Ten years later, the National Labour Union began to press for this change in the United States. It achieved some success in 1868, when the US Congress set an eight-hour day for workers involved in federal projects. By the 1880s, many unions around the world began to focus on the shorter working day as their main goal. The eight-hour day was their ideal, and 350,000 workers demonstrated for it in Chicago in 1886.

Three years later, a British union took up the cause and succeeded. In March 1889, some employees of Beckton Gas Works were laid off. Gas workers from all over London held a protest meeting. One speaker, Will Thorne, proposed a new gas workers' union to improve their working conditions. He also suggested that they concentrate on an eight-hour day rather than on a pay increase.

'I pledge my word that, if you will stand firm and don't waver, within six months we will claim and win the eight-hour day, a six-day week, and the abolition of the present slave-driving methods in vogue not only at the Beckton Gas Works, but all over the country.'

Union organizer Will Thorne, addressing a meeting of London gas workers, March 31, 1889.

Soon, more than 800 people had joined the new National Union of Gas Workers & General Labourers, with Thorne as its leader. Within a few weeks, the owners of Beckton and two other gasworks had agreed to reduce the working day from 12 hours to eight. This amazing success boosted the union movement, and the new gas workers' union soon had more than 20,000 members.

American efforts had their best early results within the government rather than in private industry. In 1892, Congress extended the eight-hour day to include all federal employees. The first national law for private industry came in 1916 with the Adamson Act, which set the eight-hour day for all railway employees (who had threatened a national strike if the change was not made). Other agreements came about as a result of negotiations between employees and specific companies or industries rather than as a result of new laws.

Working Together

A poster (right) calls for further workers' meetings in Chicago following the 'Haymarket Massacre' of 1886, when police attacked a labour rally. The poster is also in German, reflecting the number of German-speaking immigrants in the Chicago work force.

Workers' Verses

The following poem appeared in the *Ontario Workman* newspaper on May 18, 1872.

It had been passed on by word of mouth among workers in Canada and the United States:

We mean to make things over;
We're tired of toil for naught [nothing]
But bare enough to live on;
Never an hour for thought;
We want to see the sunshine,
We want to smell the flowers;
We're sure that God has willed it,
And we mean to have eight hours.
We're summoning our forces,
From shipyard, shop, and mill;
Eight hours for work,
eight hours for rest,
Eight hours for what we will!

From the factories and the workshops,
In long and weary lines,
From all the sweltering forges,
From all the sunless mines;
Wherever toil is wasting
The force of life to live;
Its bent and battered armies
Come to claim what God doth give.
And the blazon [symbol] on its banner
Doth with hope the nations fill;
Eight hours for work,
eight hours for rest,
Eight hours for what we will!

Success and Reaction

The period leading up to World War I (1914–18) saw a huge rise in union membership around the world. Britain was still the most economically powerful country in the world, thanks to its established trade links and large empire. But other countries, notably the United States and Germany, were catching up quickly. In all of these countries – as well as in Canada, Australia, and other industrial powers – organized workers were using the strike weapon successfully to achieve a wide range of goals.

The most extreme example of workers' power came with the Russian Revolution of 1917, in which **communists** led the overthrow of the Russian monarchy. With banners such as 'Workers of the World Unite', the Russian revolutionaries inspired fear and admiration in the rest of the world. Many employers and governments worried that the revolution would spill beyond Russia's borders, sweeping aside privately owned companies and leading to violence and chaos. Radical workers, on the other hand, believed that they could push for even more rights if employers feared revolution as the alternative.

Demonstrating workers flee from government troops in Petrograd (Saint Petersburg) in 1917 during the Russian Revolution.

Turmoil and Progress

The threat of revolution meant that politics had entered the union movement. The shocks of World War I, the Russian Revolution and the **Great Depression** of the 1930s brought workers' rights to centre stage in many countries. British workers in nearly every type of employment paralyzed their country by staging a general strike in 1926. The 1927 trial of Sacco and Vanzetti (see panel) reflected America's fears of the 'red menace' of communism. The Depression, which affected most of the world, hurt workers and employers alike.

Throughout this turbulent time, governments were recognizing the need to establish more rights for workers. New laws in many countries made provision for sick pay and disability allowance and set up other government programmes to help and protect workers. Together, these measures were described as the **welfare state**, since many people saw it as the government's duty to look after citizens in the workplace.

A 'town' of makeshift cabins and lean-tos outside Seattle, Washington, at the height of the Great Depression in 1934. Similar towns sprang up outside many US cities as jobless families looked for work in the cities. These unofficial communities were nicknamed 'Hoovervilles' after Herbert Hoover, who was US President at the start of the Depression in 1929.

Laws to Protect Workers

The idea of a welfare state developed in many countries in the first decades of the 20th century. Great Britain passed the National Insurance Act in 1911. The act organized a health and compensation programme paid for by contributions from employers, workers and public taxes. In 1910, several US states passed workmen's compensation laws to protect workers from the risk of unemployment due to injury. Within a decade, all but six states had such laws in place. In 1913, the US Department of Labor was established to look after the interests of American workers. Later measures in both countries expanded the government's role in supporting workers. And, based on a long-held view that educational opportunities are the key to better jobs, the United States set up the GI Bill in 1945. This bill provided educational and **vocational** training opportunities for returning soldiers of World War II (1939–45).

Sacco and Vanzetti

One of the most famous trials in American history showed how fear of communism could divide a country. In 1920, two Italian immigrants, Nicola Sacco and Bartolomeo Vanzetti, were charged with two murders in an armed robbery in Massachusetts. The only evidence against them was shaky at best: Sacco owned a pistol similar to the one used in the crime, and the two men were connected with a car linked to the robbery.

Bartolomeo Vanzetti (left) and Nicola Sacco, shortly before their execution.

Many people believed that the two men were innocent and had been arrested only because they were outspoken supporters of radical ideas about workers' rights. These arguments did not sway the judge and jury, who found the men guilty in 1927. Sacco and Vanzetti were executed, but the case continued to divide the country. Over the years, new evidence arose indicating that the two men were probably innocent of the crime. In August 1977, Massachusetts Governor Michael Dukakis signed a legal announcement clearing the names and reputations of Sacco and Vanzetti.

Success and Reaction

Ernest Bevin

One of Britain's leading figures in the struggle for workers' rights was Ernest Bevin (1881–1951). Bevin began his working life as a labourer but soon became a prominent union organizer. In 1920, he made his national reputation by calling for a standard minimum wage for British dockworkers. The following year, he established the Transport and General Workers' Union (TGWU), merging 32 smaller unions into a powerful new organization. Its strength enabled the TGWU to take the lead in the General Strike of 1926, which brought the British economy to a standstill for nine days. The strike itself failed to achieve any immediate benefits, but the country knew that the TGWU – and Bevin himself – could repeat the event if circumstances called for it.

Britain's General Strike of 1926, coming just nine years after the Russian Revolution, sent shock waves through the Western world even though the strike itself failed in its goals.

America's 'New Deal'

US President Franklin Roosevelt was elected in 1932 with a pledge to help America emerge from the economic depression that had begun in 1929. Using a series of government-funded measures, collectively known as the New Deal, he created thousands of jobs and passed a number of laws to establish and protect workers' rights. The National Labour Relations Act of 1935 created a system of fair employment practices and gave federal assistance to the wage-bargaining process. The Fair Labour Standards Act, passed three years later, set the maximum number of hours and the minimum wage for most American workers. Throughout the New Deal, Roosevelt was aided by his Secretary of Labour, Frances Perkins, who became the first female member of the US **Cabinet** in 1933.

The Wider Struggle

The campaign for rights at work had long been isolated and sporadic, with a small victory in one place being offset by a defeat elsewhere. Sometimes, apparent defeats, such as the case of the Tolpuddle Martyrs (see page 13), turned into sources of inspiration for those who carried on the struggle in other places or in other lines of work. Likewise, new employment laws passed in some countries, notably Great Britain and the United States, inspired union leaders and politicians in other countries to follow their example.

Throughout this long and uneven period of general progress, the notion of rights at work was seen as an issue in its own right. Other major struggles taking place – notably the fights for racial equality and women's suffrage (the right to vote) – occurred along separate lines. Sometimes there would be a 'crossover' from one struggle to another, with a leading proponent of women's suffrage supporting women in a strike or a local union helping its African-American members to share in the benefits of a wage-bargaining settlement. But overall, these major issues were clear-cut and separate.

Supporters of women suffrage publicize their cause at an information booth in New York City in 1914, five years before US women gained the right to vote.

United Fronts

In the decades following World War II, the issue of civil rights inspired many people in many countries to see racial equality as a necessary first step towards other areas of social improvement. People from ethnic minorities, and their supporters, struggled to achieve a 'level playing field' in the prosperous countries of the West, which meant receiving better opportunities in education, health, and housing. Other improvements in employment law would have to follow.

The British economy took many years to recover from the war, and the government encouraged immigration from Commonwealth countries. These new workers, many from the Caribbean region, faced hardships in getting good housing and their resentment was, in turn, matched by the anger of some British people who believed that their own jobs were at risk. Australia and Canada also saw widespread immigration from Asia and southern Europe. These 'newcomers' also had to press for social equality in order to find and hold down steady jobs.

More than 200,000 people joined the peaceful March on Washington in August 1963 in an effort to promote stronger civil rights laws.

The move for greater racial equality in these countries launched 'united fronts' pushing for changes in areas ranging from employment law to the environment. There were significant advances in the workplace, especially in removing discrimination against racial minorities, women, and handicapped people. Other protests laid the groundwork for new struggles that continue today. Ideas such as paternity leave for working fathers were mocked in the sixties, but have now resurfaced – and have even become law in some countries, such as Sweden.

Expanding Civil Liberties

In the second half of the 20th century, many people believed that rights at work were simply one element in a wider network of **civil liberties**. American labour leader A. Philip Randolph (1889–1979) typified this view.

Randolph grew up in Florida, where he worked on the railways as a young man. He later moved to New York City, where he became interested in union affairs – and especially the problems faced by African-American workers. While attending the College of the City of New York, he organized a union of lift operators. This union's success inspired him to return to the railways, where he had noticed ill treatment of black workers. In 1925, Randolph organized the Brotherhood of Sleeping Car Porters. This was the first union made up of mainly black workers to be granted a charter by the American Federation of Labor. After a decade, the union was recognized as the workers' bargaining agent with their main employer, the Pullman Company.

During the 1930s, Randolph became a respected voice in labour affairs, especially those that involved civil rights issues. In 1941, he persuaded President Franklin Roosevelt to set up the Fair Employment Practices Committee. This committee worked to ensure that companies doing business with the US government would not discriminate against African-Americans and other minority groups. Randolph remained committed to the civil rights movement and helped to organize the famous March on Washington in 1963.

Senator Robert Kennedy (left) shares bread with Cesar Chavez after Chavez ended a 23-day fast in support of farm workers in the US in 1968.

People Power

Mass marches in the 1960s helped bring about a spirit of cooperation that involved ordinary people in ways that had never been the case before. Supporters of civil rights causes also saw that they could influence events with their choice of what to buy and what to leave on the store shelves. This type of 'people power' became an important weapon in the campaign of the National Farm Workers Association in the United States. In 1968 its leader Cesar Chavez organized a boycott of California grapes which helped to secure official union contracts for its mainly Hispanic farm workers. Similar boycotts of goods and services worked on an international level. Campaigners in the UK, Australia and other countries, added economic pressure to protests aimed at overturning South Africa's racist policies.

Too Much Power?

Events such as the 1972 miners' strike in Great Britain (see panel) and reports of corruption in some American unions turned many people away from the labour movement in the late 1970s. The mood in many countries was becoming more conservative, and there was talk – especially in Britain – of governments being 'held at ransom' by too-powerful unions.

This wave of anti-union feeling was reflected in the election of Margaret Thatcher as British prime minister in 1979 and of Ronald Reagan as US president in 1980. Each of these leaders came to power with the promise of giving power 'back to the people'. In previous decades, that phrase almost certainly would have meant giving power to ordinary working people. But in the new political climate, it meant taking power from the working people's unions. One of President Reagan's first acts in office was to crush an air traffic controllers' strike in 1981, leaving no room for compromise. Prime Minister Thatcher faced an even bigger battle in 1984, when the powerful National Union of Mineworkers, which had been responsible for the crippling 1972 strike, went on strike again. This time, however, the strike ended with a humiliating defeat for the miners and their combative leader, Arthur Scargill.

Britain in the Dark

Few events affected British anti-union opinion in the 1970s as much as the Miners' Strike of 1972. On January 9, 1972, Britain's coal miners went on strike for the first time in 50 years, demanding a 36-per cent pay increase. Nearly all of Britain's mines were owned by the government, which had set an eight-per cent limit on pay increases. Within days, Britain's stockpiles of coal began to dwindle. With coal supplies – essential to produce much of Britain's electricity – running low, the government was forced to take drastic measures to save electricity. Power plants had to cut electric supplies for up to nine hours a day, and the government imposed a three-day working week on the entire country. Many shops and other businesses tried to operate in the winter darkness with only candles and oil lamps to light them.

The strike – with its damaging consequences – eventually had an effect. On February 9, the government declared a **state of emergency**. Two days later, it set up a special commission to investigate the miners' demands. Representatives of the miners' union and the government struggled to reach a compromise. Eventually, on February 19, a deal was made. The miners received a large pay increase, although not as large as they had demanded. However, the union claimed that the miners had extracted 15 other concessions from the government.

There is no exact answer to who 'won' the 1972 miners' strike. But the memory of dark, unheated buildings and people forced to work and earn less because of the strike remained strong for many British people. It was this memory that helped Margaret Thatcher (pictured) get elected in 1979 with a promise to reduce the power of unions. In her first four years in power, her government did just that.

Still a Weapon

Despite the disillusionment that many **Western** people felt towards unions and their power, other countries showed that unions still had massive support. Ironically, the best examples came from communist countries whose political systems were supposed to safeguard workers' rights. The first big move against communist power came in Poland in late 1980, when shipyard workers in the port of Gdansk organized an unofficial union called Solidarity. Led by Lech Walesa, Solidarity defied the government with demonstrations and work stoppages. By early 1981, it had more than 13 million members across Poland. Throughout the 1980s, Solidarity operated **underground**, gradually becoming more powerful. By 1989, the communist government was forced to agree to a free election and, in 1990, Walesa was elected president of Poland.

In the late 1980s, students and workers in communist China also mounted large demonstrations against the government and in favour of democracy. The biggest of these, in the heart of Beijing in June 1989, was crushed by the army, but the government has since had to allow workers more individual freedoms.

Polish voters recalled the efforts of Lech Walesa and his Solidarity union when they elected him president in 1990 a year after the fall of communism in Poland.

38

Too Much Power

Player power

Professional sports are industries, just like manufacturing or farming, and like these other industries, they also have disputes. European football was shaken up in 1990 when a Belgian player, Jean-Marc Bosman chose to move to the French side Dunkerque because his contract had run out. His Belgian club, Liege, refused because Dunkerque did not offer a large enough transfer fee. Bosman took his case to the European Court of Justice, which ruled – five years later – in his favour. The decision meant that any footballer was free to use a 'free transfer' to another EU-based team at the end of his contract.

Such a profound dispute can rock an entire sport. Baseball, known as 'America's pastime', has had two strikes after the players' union, the Major League Players' Association (MLPA) clashed with owners. The issue at stake was similar to the heart of the Bosman conflict, whether players could become free agents in search of the best pay.

A Beijing protester stands in the path of tanks as the Chinese government crushes a massive demonstration in Tiananmen Square on June 5, 1989.

Rewriting the Rules

The Industrial Revolution, beginning more than two centuries ago, changed the way people worked in nearly every country. In doing so, it also changed the way people – both employers and employees – lived. Replacing old working practices with new ones altered the landscape, created the demand for new skills and revolutionized notions of when, where, and how people would work. It also sowed the seeds for the first systematic campaign to improve working conditions.

The new century sees the world in the midst of what is sometimes called the 'communications revolution' or the 'technological revolution'. Traditional forms of manufacturing are in decline as machines, and even robots, replace human workers. In place of manufacturing are many examples of what is called the service economy, employing people in the computing industry, fast-food restaurants and many jobs that did not even exist two or three decades ago. Many people even work from home, linked to other workers through Internet connections.

An engineer uses his computer to inspect a partially built automobile at a Ford Motor factory in Ontario, Canada.

Thousands of protesters against globalization (the increased power of huge companies around the world) demonstrate on the last day of the World Social Forum in Porto Alegre, Brazil in January 2005.

Empowerment

One of the buzzwords of modern social thinking is 'empowerment'. We hear of groups or individuals being empowered at school, in the workplace or in the wider world. The principle is simple. Most people who are denied certain opportunities – for example, to rights at work or to work itself – would prefer to improve their position on their own. Empowering such people means removing some of the obstacles they face so that they can do just that.

The Campaign for Labor Rights (CLR), an international organization, states that its goal is to empower workers. Based in the United States, it seeks to promote economic and social justice by campaigning to end labour rights violations around the world. First, the group educates people in rich, consumer countries about the unfair practices that keep the prices of shoes, shirts, footballs and other goods low. Many of these items are produced in **sweatshops**. CLR hopes people will think twice about buying some of these products until the companies change their practices. The group's second strategy is to provide the same information about sweatshop practices to the United Nations (UN) and other international organizations. These organizations can often put pressure on governments to force changes in working practices.

New Goals

Unions no longer have the national influence they once wielded in many countries, and most of them have far fewer members than in previous decades. Imaginative labour leaders, however, know that there is always room for improvement in the workplace, especially in an era when so much is changing. Few workers have the taste for the long, damaging strikes – often for increased pay – that were so common in the past.

UAW President Walter Reuther addresses a group of low-income Americans in 1966.

One of the first union leaders to grasp the importance of non-wage goals was Walter Reuther, president of United Automobile Workers of America (UAW). Reuther established the UAW as a powerful bargaining agent at both Ford and General Motors in the 1930s and 1940s. Although he organized successful sit-down strikes at Ford, Reuther was a moderate who believed in building trust between employers and workers. As leader, he turned the union's goals away from straightforward battles over pay and focused instead on profit sharing, pension plans and more holidays. He also used his influence as union leader to champion the causes of civil rights, affordable housing and environmental protection.

Many of the existing labour laws – such as injury compensation for industrial accidents – are far less relevant today than they were two centuries ago. But that does not mean that there are no longer problems in the workplace. Instead, it means that workers and employers must examine life in the 'new economy' and find ways to ensure that workers today are treated fairly.

The Role of Education

One way to ensure that people enjoy the best possible rights at work is to provide them with the chance to do the job that best suits them. That means offering people the best educational opportunities to excel in different fields. It was this view that inspired 19th century educational reformers such as George Birkbeck. He established the London Mechanic's Institute (now Birkbeck College) to help provide working-class men with educational opportunities. Mechanic's institutes sprang up elsewhere in Britain, giving people the chance to 'improve themselves' and helping to pave the way for more widespread reforms such as the Education Act of 1870.

Today, educational reformers are still at work, and many of them have an international focus. International organizations such as the Global Campaign for Education help promote literacy and higher educational opportunities for schoolchildren around the world. They help countries build for the future by educating their most precious natural resource – children.

Students at a public school in Ethiopia in 2002. They are the future of a country that has suffered decades of hunger and civil war.

What's Next?

Many of the triumphs in the field of workers' rights have been achieved in the richest countries of the world, such as Great Britain, the United States, Canada, and Australia. But these same countries have entered a new phase of their development, sometimes called the 'new economy' (see pages 40–41) or the 'postindustrial economy' because fewer products are being manufactured at home. Nevertheless, people in rich consumer countries are still buying manufactured goods, even if many of them are not produced in their own factories.

Pakistani children working at an embroidery factory in 2003. Child labour remains a serious problem in many parts of the world.

Today, many goods are produced in **developing countries**, which have established their own factories. Some of these new manufacturing countries have not shared in the fight for rights at work. Their workers face some of the same conditions – including child labour – that so horrified 19th-century social reformers. For example, working conditions in many parts of Latin America, India and Southeast Asia remain poor, and there are few regulations to protect the rights of employees.

Thus, the fight for workers' rights is far from over. As nations struggle to find their place in the 21st century, more must be done to ensure that workers in every country are protected from the wide range of threats to rights in the workplace.

International Involvement

Many of the first organizers of trade unions saw a future in which international unions would look after the interests of members from every country. The gains achieved by members in one country would be transferred easily to working practices in other nations. That system never developed, however. Although some international unions do exist, they operate mainly as a way of exchanging information. There is little or no legal power to spread working agreements from one country to another.

There are, however, other ways of spreading the gains throughout the world. Several of these methods operate within the framework of the United Nations, which has served as a forum for international cooperation for nearly six decades. The UN seeks to improve the conditions of people living and working in all of its member countries, especially those in the developing world. Special projects focus on health, education and farming to provide the basic structure each country needs to support its people.

The UN body that deals with employment is the International Labour Organization (ILO). The ILO is not exactly a trade union. Instead, it helps unions around the world communicate and cooperate with each other. It sets guidelines that countries should strive to follow in their working practices and investigates some of the worst abuses workers face. As part of the United Nations (on which many governments rely for funding), the ILO can help put pressure on countries to comply with these guidelines.

US President Bill Clinton signs an international agreement on world trade in 1993.

Glossary and Suggested Reading

boycott   the refusal to do business with a person or company as a form of protest

Cabinet   the group of senior ministers in the national government

call centres   centres for answering telephone calls made to a company

carters   people who make or repair wagon wheels

Chartists   supporters of the People's Charter, a British movement for increased political representation for workers that led to a series of protests from 1838 to 1848

civil liberties   basic individual rights, such as freedom of speech and freedom of religion

civil rights   basic human rights ensuring that all citizens of a country receive the same treatment

collective bargaining   negotiations between workers' representatives and an employer

communists   people who support a type of government in which the state (government) owns all properties and businesses

consumers   people or countries that buy and use (consume) manufactured goods

developing countries   countries that rely on basic farming rather than on developed industries for their income

feudal system   a system of government in Medieval Europe in which farm labourers worked for wealthy landowners in return for military protection

Great Depression   a period, roughly from 1929 to 1939, during which the world economy declined, causing millions of people to lose their jobs

Hispanic   of or from a country with a Spanish-speaking culture

illiterate   unable to read or write

indentured servants   people bound by contract to work for someone else for a set period

Industrial Revolution   a period in the late 18th and 19th centuries when there were rapid advances in manufacturing techniques

job security   the knowledge that a person can keep a job for a long time if he or she wants to do so

Middle Ages   a period of European history, often dated from the 5th to the 15th centuries

minorities   people who are part of a group that is less than half of a larger group

mutinied   refused to follow the orders of a commander

paternity leave   absence allowed a father who takes time off work to look after a baby

peasants   farm workers who rented land from landowners

pensions   regular allowances paid to people when they retire from work

philanthropic   providing help as a form of charity

provident   providing for future events or needs

...ical   favouring widespread and immediate changes to a political system

...affold   a platform from which condemned people were hanged

state of emergency   a time when a government suspends some individual freedoms in order to concentrate on solving an unexpected, dramatic problem

stockyards   enclosed yards where livestock are kept until they are sold or slaughtered

sweatshops   factories in which low-paid workers work in difficult conditions

telecommuting   working at home or somewhere else away from other workers and connected to them via telephone or computer

textile   a woven cloth or fabric

underground   unofficially and out of the sight of police or security forces

union   a group of people sharing a type of work or employer who band together to press for improved working conditions

vocational   having to do with skilled trades such as plumbing or carpentry

welfare state   a political system in which the government assumes responsibility for the population

Western   countries that rejected communism and allowed individuals to own businesses and property

workhouse   an institution where unemployed paupers were housed at public expense

Suggested Reading

Stearman, Kay. *Just the Facts: Child Labour.* Oxford: Heinemann, 2004.

Trades Union Congress. *The Tolpuddle Martyrs: The story of the Martyrs told through contemporary accounts, letters and documents.* London: Trades Union Congress, 2000.

Grant, Joan (ed.) *The Australopedia: How Australia works after 200 years of other people living here.* Fitzroy, Victoria: McPhee Gribble/Penguin, 1988

Web sites

Spartacus Educational Website (British labour history)
www.spartacus.schoolnet.co.uk/REVhistoryTU.htm
Tolpuddle Martyrs Museum
www.tolpuddlemartyrs.org.uk
Trades Union Congress union history (UK)
www.unionhistory.info/
Working Lives (Australian labour history)
www.econ.usyd.edu.au/wos/workinglives

Index